Kauai

She is the oldest of Hawaii's main islands, but Kauai wears her age with undeniably rare beauty and charm. Lush rainforests, exotic flora, and cascading waterfalls have well earned her the title "The Garden Isle."

Beyond her luxuriant landscape lies the grandeur of Waimea Canyon—a living panorama of nature's hues, and untouched wilderness.

Kauai's crowning glory is her lei of beaches. The glistening white sands and brilliant blue waters are truly a captivating lure for sunbathers and water enthusiasts alike. Embraced by the majestic Na Pali Cliffs, Kauai's picturesque north shore offers secluded beaches—a private "paradise" hidden from all but those who boat or hike in.

In all its tropical splendor this magnificent island captures you . . . and enraptures you. Charisma . . . beauty . . .enchantment — Kauai.

*Helicopters provide an
exquisite view of the
Na Pali coast*

SIGHTSEEING

HANAKAPIAI is just one of the many valleys accessible from a hiking trail that begins at Kee Beach.

A rare double rainbow crowns the majestic NA PALI cliffs.

*HANALEI VALLEY taro
fields make an exquisite
backdrop for any photograph.*

Open to visitors, the KILAUEA LIGHTHOUSE oversees the sapphire-blue Pacific.

PRINCEVILLE is widely known for its excellent golf as well as tennis and horseback riding.

Lush tropical foliage is one reason the FERN GROTTO is a visitor favorite.

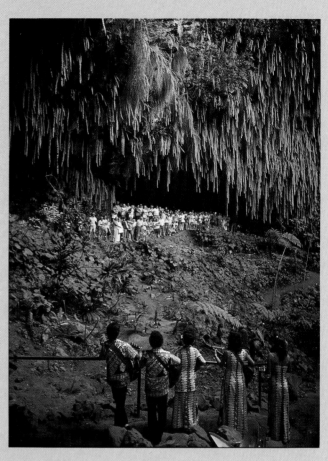

The popular torch-lighting ceremony can be seen in the early evening at many resorts.

The view of OPAEKAA FALLS explains Kauai's nickname "The Garden Isle."

Lavender water lilies are a
beautiful example of the
unique flora found on the island.

A riverboat winds its way
along the WAILUA RIVER to
the Fern Grotto.

An early morning mist adds a feeling of fantasy to the elegance of *WAILUA FALLS.*

A frosty and flavorful shave ice is an island favorite for cooling off.

Giant eucalyptus form a near mile long TREE TUNNEL on the road to Koloa and Poipu.

The MENEHUNE FISH-POND is said to have been built in one night by the menehune, a legendary race of playful Hawaiian elves.

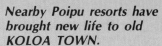

Nearby Poipu resorts have brought new life to old *KOLOA TOWN.*

A tranquil view of *KOLOA MILL,* part of Hawaii's oldest plantation founded in 1835.

Crystal blue waters turn into power-ful geysers in the SPOUTING HORN lava tube.

An occasional mist creates rainbows over WAIMEA CANYON.

Often called "a miniature Grand Canyon," WAIMEA CANYON is a magnificent site all its own.

A Kokee State Park lookout gives an unparalleled view of an emerald green KALALAU VALLEY.

KALALAU VALLEY gets its share of misty rainbows.

WAIMEA CANYON'S west rim provides a striking sunset.

The road to Kauai's north shore ends at KEE BEACH, where reef-sheltered waters offer ideal swimming and diving.

Zodiak rafts carry passengers to isolated NA PALI coast beaches.

BEACHES

Uncrowded coves with brilliant turquoise waters make LUMAHAI BEACH one of the island's most photogenic.

The reef-lined shores and crystal blue waters of Kauai are ideal for snorkeling.

The perfect mile-long crescent coast of HANALEI BAY.

Afternoon sailors love Kauai's gentle breezes and inviting waters.

Sunbathers and swimmers thrive on the still uncrowded shores of POIPU BEACH.

Nawiliwili Harbor meets the shore of KALAPAKI BEACH.

KAPAA BEACH is just one of many that lure visitors from around the world.